You Can Prophesy!

A Prophetic Pocket-Guide of Proven Strategies and
Instructions on How to Release Personal and Corporate
Prophecy

Dwann Holmes Rollinson

Sermon To Book
www.sermontobook.com

You Can Prophesy! / Dwann Rollinson
ISBN-13: 9780692571439
ISBN-10: 0692571434

You Can Prophesy *is dedicated to all of my prophetic students and mentees who have come through The Global Institute of Church & Marketplace Prophets, as well as to those spiritual sons and daughters who understand what I mean when I say Prophesy, Prophet; Prophesy!*

Yes, as a Prophet, at the very least you should be able to prophesy. But more than anything, as a believer you should be able to edify, exhort, and comfort others through Prophecy. No matter who you are in the Kingdom, You Can Prophesy!

CONTENTS

Foreword

You Can Prophesy does several very vital things for the Body of Christ today. Chief among them is that it validates one of the most advantageous reasons God put His Holy Spirit within us, which is to let us hear Him speak. Another reason we have the Holy Spirit within us is to speak for Him.

In a world where every other deity has a voice and a body of people to publish their god's thoughts, it just makes good sense that the God of gods should have the same, and He does. *You Can Prophesy* proves it, and goes into intelligent discussion on how to speak out loud what your God says from inside you. So why is it so important that the children of God accept that they can prophesy? The answer is because God speaks. From the moment He said, "Let there be light," He has never stopped speaking and He will continue to talk out loud to this world as long as it exists. The drawback is that His voice is inaudible to the average person on earth and needs amplification to be heard, and sometimes translation to be understood. This is because most natural people cannot equally hear from a supernatural voice. So God sent the Holy Spirit into the world to be His amplifier, He enables seekers to find and hear from Him.

People crave to hear from God and race here and there to obtain tomorrow's answers today. It prepares and arms them to take on life and succeed more often than they fail. They need us to pray for them, but they also need us to hear for them too at times. In the same way you can approach God in prayer, you who have Him on the inside of you can petition Him for wisdom. That is what prophesying is above all else, the wisdom of God voiced in this world. Now, as for teaching people to prophesy, this question has been the stumbling block to many a voice of God, so here are some things to consider.

Preachers are taught to preach, teachers are taught to teach, worshippers are taught to sing and praise, and leaders are taught to lead. These ministers too have the Lord's Spirit within them and still, to be excellent and accurate, they are taught, no matter how talented or gifted they may be. When it comes to prophesying, consider this. Before any of them existed, the Lord taught prophets to prophesy and priests to hear and reveal His thoughts. Since He is the same yesterday, today, and forever, He assigns modern teachers in His body to equip others to hear and serve Him because people are born not knowing things. Despite how deeply they feel them they require something (or someone) to bridge the gap between what they feel, what they think, and what they can speak out. That is the work of teaching and training. It is why this book presents some practical ways "you can prophesy."

Lastly, is the question of what prophecy is exactly. Prophecy is God answering in this world what He wants us to act on. Sometimes His answers predict, sometimes they correct. Sometimes they enlighten and at other times they soothe, guide, or comfort. Whichever one it is, the real joy we as His family on earth share is that He speaks to us, a high honor that so many others on the planet miss. We Christians are privileged to hear the Almighty's voice and share His thoughts. Nothing on earth tops either of these. So yes, *You Can Prophesy*. Just take the time to learn how to prophesy well. Respect your gift enough to be accurate and you will declare the word of the Lord confidently.

Paula A. Price, PhD
Author – The Prophet's Dictionary &
The Prophet's Handbook
Founder – N.E.A.R. Apostleship Restitution

You Can Prophesy!

Introduction

One of the most controversial prophetic topics I seem to encounter weekly is whether or not I can teach someone to prophesy.

I never would have imagined that so many "Bible-believing" Christians literally believe that one form of Prophecy can't be taught because it is a Spiritual Gift.

This completely baffles me.

It's as if these same closed-minded folks wouldn't be able to comprehend how someone with the gift of a great singing voice should surely practice and could probably increase their ability to use their gift if they did so regularly. Especially with specialized training from one who has the grace and gift to help them increase in that area.

Essentially, that's what I tend to explain more than I care to, to folks across the world.

Many times, they are confused, whether they know it or not, about the gift of Prophecy versus the Kingdom Agent of the Prophet.

They have no idea how many prophets and prophetic people I come across who yearn for help with the release and delivery of prophecy, one-on-one and corporately.

They have no idea how many prophets I interact with who clearly have a prophetic stream, but who haven't been taught how to maximize flowing in that prophetic stream.

And they certainly have no idea of the amount of believers I have successfully helped with this.

I remember all the passionate discussion that came forth when I began to advertise one of my most popular webinars, from which this guidebook has been developed, entitled *Teach Me How to Prophesy.*

I chuckle as I write this.

You would have thought I had shot a video cursing folks out, the way some reacted.

They were adamant even as they posed questions developed to manipulate a certain response.

They asked: "Aren't gifts given By God?"

To which I answered: "Of course!"

Yet that doesn't negate the fact that even if God has given us gifts, it is still up to us to take responsibility for that gift and for going from level to level and glory to glory with that same gift.

Otherwise we could essentially end up like the servants who hid and buried the talent(s) that their master left for them.

When the master left each of his servants the talents, he expected them to multiply what was given to them.

He expected them to be strategic in using those talents for future glory.

I believe that this is what God expects when He blesses us with spiritual gifts and natural talent.

However, the stream of prophecy that I will address in these pages should be more closely associated with the gift of prophetic prayer.

I say this because I know from experience that if you can think of it from this perspective, you will be able to benefit better because you will more easily come out of agreement with the false belief that "teaching prophecy" can't be done.

In the Bible, we see the disciples specifically request that Jesus teach them how to pray.

In the New International Version of the Bible, it reads like this:

"One day Jesus was praying in a certain place. When he finished, one of his disciples said to him, 'Lord, teach us to pray, just as John taught his disciples.'"

I propose, just as the disciples asked, we too can request: TEACH ME HOW TO PROPHESY. At that moment, we will transition to another level of learning simply because we are willing to admit that we want more, and we want God or the teachers He sends our way to impart more through the gift of teaching.

So whether or not you are one who is able to prophesy at any time or one who thinks you have to pray in tongues for several minutes before you prophesy, I challenge you right now to take God outside of the box you may have put him in based on your former experiences—and quite frankly your former foundational teachings.

If you are reading this right now, I don't believe it is an accident.

I believe God has ordained this moment in time through providence. You see, He knows where you are in Him and what it will take for you to truly get to the next level of manifesting destiny in your life with the prophetic call that is upon your life.

Whether you're a teenager or a seasoned saint, if you take this guidebook seriously and explicitly follow the instructions, I believe you will immediately see an increase in your prophetic life.

With this in mind, I prophesy that as you read the pages of this guidebook, your spiritual eyes will be opened and the weight of the prophetic in you shall be increased without strain!

Receive it today and know without a shadow of a doubt: You CAN Prophesy!

Let's Get Started

God has given me a passion to educate, enlighten, and empower prophetic intercessors, prophetic worshippers, and prophets in training. One of the ways I do this is via the Global Institute of Church and Marketplace Prophets.

This book is for prophets and prophetic people who want a clear understanding of how to accurately and boldly prophesy into a person's life one-on-one, and in a corporate environment as well. This book is for prophetic people who really want to increase the prophetic inside them by understanding what prophecy is and what prophecy isn't from a biblical perspective.

This is for those dreamers, seers, and prophets who want to confidently stand before the people of God and proclaim the Word of the Lord and know that they haven't conjured something up in the spirit.

Take a moment to ponder these questions:

- Are you tired of clamming up every time someone in leadership asks you to give the Word of the Lord for the ministry or for your church?

- Are you confident that God is speaking to you, but fear that you will say the wrong thing and cause a person's destiny to be detoured?

- Are you tired of getting vague answers about how to concisely speak into a person's life on a personal level?

- Have you ever been around a seasoned prophet who prophesied into someone's life for fifteen minutes or more, and in your mind you told yourself, *there is no way in the world I will ever be able to do that?*

- Are you dreaming detailed dreams, but lack the understanding to convert them into the Word of the Lord?

- Is there a gap between where you *are* in the prophetic and where you *need* to be?

- Do you want to know for *sure* that you understand what it means to prophesy?

- Do you sometimes feel like you just don't know if what God is saying to you is true?

In this book, you will learn that there is a clear way to tap into the Holy Spirit at any given moment and be confident in what God wants you to say to anyone at any time and any place. Does that sound like the kind of book you'd like to read? If you answered with a resounding "yes" to any of the questions, then you will enjoy this read.

This biblical system, if you will, involves more than just praying in the Spirit and hoping to hit the prophetic mark.

I want you to know, dear reader, that everything I teach in this book is all based on the questions I get asked before, during, and after prophetic ministry. I do not know everything on the subject of prophecy—not even close—but I do have many experiences, tips, and words of encouragement to share. With that, let's get started.

What Will This Book Cover?

- The basics of prophecy

- How to release a prophetic word for a person

- How to release a prophetic word for a corporate gathering

- Practical applications

- Q&A

PART ONE

The Basics of Prophecy

Pursue love, and earnestly desire the spiritual gifts, especially that you may prophecy. For one who speaks in a tongue speaks not to men but to God; for no one understands him, but he utters mysteries in the Spirit. On the other hand, the one who prophesies speaks to people for their upbuilding and encouragement and consolation. — 1 Corinthians 14:1-4

The NIV says it this way:

Anyone who speaks in a tongue edifies themselves, but the one who prophesies edifies the church. I would like every one of you to speak in tongues, but I would rather have you prophesy. — 1 Corinthians 14:4-5

The key scripture is found in verse 5:

I would like every one of you to speak in tongues, but I would rather have you prophesy. The one who prophesies is greater than the one who speaks in tongues, unless someone interprets, so that the church may be edified. — 1 Corinthians 14:5 (NIV)

According to this passage of scripture, the one who prophesies is greater than the one who speaks in tongues, unless someone interprets so that the church may be edified. When you have a chance in your spare time, study 1 Corinthians 14.

What is the Purpose of Prophecy?

- To edify (i.e., build up, lift up, establish, or strengthen).

- To exhort (i.e., urge, advise, caution earnestly, or admonish urgently).

- To comfort (i.e., soothe, console, or reassure and bring cheer).

What Prophecy Is Not

Prophecy is not a way to make people:

- Doubt God

- Doubt their destiny

- Doubt what God has spoken to them in the past

- Belittle, embarrass, or harass

- Confuse, scare, or intimidate

If any of these situations occur, know that the message is not of God, is not biblical, nor is it true prophecy. *Then what is it?* Answer: It's of the flesh.

How to Release Basic Prophecy

How does one release basic prophecy? It's very simple: through the Word of God. So, whether you're a prophetic intercessor, prophetic worshipper, a seasoned prophet, or a prophet in training, the number one way to boost your prophetic gift is to consistently study the Word of God. Why? Because it will increase the accuracy and clarity of your prophetic messages.

Your next question might be: "Once I receive my prophetic Word, how do I release it in a God-honoring and accurate way?" Excellent question.

Right now I'm going to give you some one-on-one starting points, and then—based on the Word that God has given you—I want you to expand the prophecy in a notebook. This is an actual activity that I want you to stop and do. Ready? Go.

One-on-One Sample Starting Points

Sample Starting Point 1: Let's say you know someone who is going through a divorce. How are you going to minister to them? Start with scripture passages that you know apply to their particular situation.

Then, by way of comfort, say something like, "God says He is going to supply all of your needs according to His riches in heaven."

Next thing you know, your prophecy is being released. But please note: It's up to you to come up with the initial scripture passage that applies to their unique situation. Then, you must wait for your prophetic message to come.

Take Five Minutes: What kind of scriptures do you think apply to someone who is going through a divorce? Write down your answers.

Sample Starting Point 2: Let's say you know a new business owner. Take a moment to think of scriptures that are going to apply to this person, who most likely needs to be edified and possibly exhorted. They are walking in faith, believing that they are going to earn enough money to quit their current job.

I might tell them: "God says He has given you the power to earn wealth."

Take Five Minutes: What kind of scriptures do you think apply to a new business owner? Write down your answers.

Sample Starting Point 3: Let's say you know someone who has recently lost their spouse. It's very difficult to minister to those who have lost loved ones, but there are ways to comfort, to soothe, to console, to reassure, and to bring cheer.

I might say: "Scripture says to be absent from the body is to be present with the Lord. God says that He's never going to leave you or forsake you, even during this tragic time."

Take Five Minutes: What kind of scriptures do you think apply to a widow? Write down your answers.

Sample Starting Point 4: Let's say you know someone who is going through emotional distress. You sense oppression, you sense sadness, but you really don't know why. I might say something like, "The Word of the Lord says the joy of the Lord is your strength."

Take Five Minutes: What kind of scriptures do you think apply to someone who is going through emotional distress? Write down your answers.

Remember, no matter what prophetic situation you are in, you should always be relying on the Word of God, not your flesh or your mind. Your whole goal in prophesying is to simply release basic prophecy from the Word of the Lord.

The Next Level of Prophecy

Now I'm going to give you the spiritual definition of prophecy. This is coming from the *Prophet's Dictionary* written by Dr. Paula Price. Prophecy is an inspired communication from God. This occurs when you are clearly a prophetic intercessor, a seasoned prophet, or even a prophet-in-training. You sense God releasing something upon you that needs to be released to the person, but you're going to start with the Word of God and then you're going to see what God says.

What Makes It Prophecy?

Prophecy occurs when God speaks through His prophets before the earthly events in question occur. In other words, predictive revelation that God, who is eternal, speaks from outside of time through His creation and family in time. Again, this definition is from the *Prophet's Dictionary.*

As humans, we are in time; God is outside of time. But He speaks to us outside of time, in time. I love that! But not everyone should be trying to flow in this, because even as seasoned prophets, we are prone to making mistakes.

You never want to put yourself in a situation where you're prophesying to somebody, but you're completely off because you're not following protocol.

So, again, the basic protocol for prophecy is releasing the Word of God. And the good news is, the entire body of Christ can participate in this form of prophesying. Its primary goal is to edify, to exhort, and to comfort.

The next level of prophecy involves inspired communication from God and typically happens during intense times of prophetic prayer, worship, dreams, and visions.

But no matter what level of prophecy you experience, there must always be a biblical foundation to build upon.

How to Corporately Release Prophecy

During this section, we're going to hone in on 2 Chronicles 20. I love the whole book of 2 Chronicles. In fact, the foundation of my ministry is built upon it, particularly 2 Chronicles 20:20, which says: "Believe in the Lord your God and you shall be established. Believe his prophets and you shall prosper."

Now let's talk about how to release a corporate prophecy.

> All the men of Judah, with their wives and children and little ones, stood there before the Lord. Then the Spirit of the Lord came on Jahaziel son of Zechariah, the son of Benaiah, the son of Jeiel, the son of Mattaniah, a Levite and descendant of Asaph, as he stood in the assembly. He said: "Listen, King Jehoshaphat and all who live in Judah and Jerusalem! This is what the Lord says to you: 'Do not be afraid or discouraged because of this vast army. For the battle is not yours, but God's. Tomorrow march down against them. They will be climbing up by the Pass of Ziz, and you will find them at the end of the gorge in the Desert of Jeruel. You will not have to fight this battle. Take up your positions; stand firm and see the deliverance the Lord will give you, Judah and Jerusalem. Do not be afraid; do not be discouraged. Go out to face them tomorrow, and the Lord will be with you.'" Jehoshaphat bowed down with his face to the ground, and all the people of Judah and Jerusalem fell down in worship before the

Lord. Then some Levites from the Kohathites and Korahites stood up and praised the Lord, the God of Israel, with a very loud voice. Early in the morning they left for the Desert of Tekoa. As they set out, Jehoshaphat stood and said, "Listen to me, Judah and people of Jerusalem! Have faith in the Lord your God and you will be upheld; have faith in his prophets and you will be successful." — **2 Chronicles 20:13-20 (NIV)**

If you really examine this scripture, you will see that certain things happened before a corporate Word was released. You will see that there was worship going on and that they were seeking God for specific answers. And if you study the Word that was being released, you will see that there is edification, exhortation, and comfort, yet specific direction that allowed the people of God to prosper in a certain area. So in this instance, the Word of God is allowing them to prosper against their enemies and to know what needs to be done or should be done so that they can prosper in what God has already established.

But, again, this is coming because there was a certain way of worshipping taking place. And it is during intense times of worship that the Spirit of God will fall.

When it comes to releasing prophecy, there's going to be some sort of standard indication that God is speaking to you on a regular basis. This normally happens with prophets and prophetic intercessors. There's something that happens and you realize that God is trying to release something or wants to release something through you.

I want you to notice that in verse 15 there's edification, exhortation, and comfort:

This is what the Lord says to you: "Do not be afraid or discouraged because of this vast army. For the battle is not yours, but God's." — 2 Chronicles 20:15 (NIV)

Then in verse 16 comes the instruction:

Tomorrow march down against them. They will be climbing up by the Pass of Ziz, and you will find them at the end of the gorge in the Desert of Jeruel. — 2 Chronicles 20:16 (NIV)

This is the prospering part of the prophetic word that's coming forth: *You will not have to fight this battle. Take up your positions; stand firm and see the deliverance the Lord will give you.*

But then here we go again at the end with more edification and comfort: "Do not be discouraged. Go out to face them tomorrow, and the Lord will be with you."

And, again, this is a model of prophecy, no matter what is happening. So this tells me that even if I prophesy to a person one-on-one and I release a basic Word of the Lord, then *that same model* should also be implemented as corporate prophecy. We're taking the same thing and expanding it to what God is speaking to us.

As God is communicating to you, He may be showing you a vision, but you will still need to find the biblical application so that you can connect the dots and release it and still provide edification, exhortation, and comfort.

PART TWO

Rana's Dream

Behold! I tell you a mystery. We shall not all sleep, but we shall all be changed, in a moment, in the twinkling of an eye, at the last trumpet. For the trumpet will sound, and the dead will be raised imperishable, and we shall be changed. — *1 Corinthians 15:51-52*

Below is an interview I had with a woman named Rana, who shared her dream with me.

RANA SPEAKING

I was in a place out of this world. I saw people, but they looked different, like porcelain dolls. They had perfect features. Then the Holy Spirit revealed to me that these people were in their glorified bodies.

As I walked further, they were smiling and were very friendly. I encountered a woman, and together we walked further to a forest. I heard a choir singing and worshipping. The woman and I were hand-in-hand, and we too were worshiping and singing for God. Then all of a sudden, showers started to pour down on me as I worshipped. It felt so good and peaceful. This place felt so beautiful and peaceful. I had no worries whatsoever.

As I walked further, the woman left and a young boy came up to me, held my hand, and we went to stand in a line. I asked him, "What is this place? Where are we?" He replied, "There is a name for this place in the Bible."

> *When it was my turn to meet him, there was a black curtain covering the area. I sat there, waiting for it to be unveiled.*

Then he spoke a name, only it was in a different language, the language of tongues. As we were standing in line in front of a building, I saw a bronze-colored man sitting in a chair looking through a window. I asked the boy, "Who is that?" He said it was the master. But he said I could only see the master through the glass window.

When it was my turn to meet him, there was a black curtain covering the area. I sat there, waiting for it to be unveiled. Then the voice of the Holy Spirit said, "If you open up the curtain, you shall surely die." Then I felt myself immediately flying out of the place before the curtain opened and I awoke.

PROPHETESS DWANN SPEAKING

What did you sense when you awoke? Did any scriptures come to mind?

RANA SPEAKING

No, the only thing I was thinking when I woke up was, *should I be scared?* Then I started thinking about how I was feeling when I was in that place. It was so peaceful. I wasn't even thinking about earth or life in this world or anything like that. So I just started to rethink those moments—the showers, the choir singing—and it became more peaceful as I was thinking. But no scriptures came to mind.

PROPHETESS DWANN SPEAKING

I'm confident that you had a heavenly experience. Never doubt that. Remember, Paul said, "I don't know whether I was caught up in the spirit or whether I was on earth." To me, this is definitely one of those types of situations. Remember, the resurrected body is a glorified body. And where are the glorified bodies going to be? In heaven.

Your heavenly experience is very similar to what I've heard from other seasoned prophets and ministers of the gospel who have actually been caught up in heaven.

The next step would be to pray over your dream. Ask God to reveal to you what scriptures may apply to your dream, why He is releasing it to you now, and what He wants you to release to the body of Christ.

> *When you step on a flower, the flower springs back up because there is no death or darkness. It's all light.*

Scriptures say that our glorified bodies will be raised in glory and in power. And the other experiences that I've heard from heaven are that when you're up in heaven there is no pain.

When you step on a flower, the flower springs back up because there is no death or darkness. It's all light. And when you are in His presence, you can't look directly on Him because the light of His presence is too powerful.

So you could definitely turn your dream into a Word of comfort for the people of God. Go find scriptures that apply. You might do a word search on the glorified body. For example, 1 Corinthians 15:58 says:

> *Therefore, my beloved brothers, be steadfast, immovable, always abounding in the work of the Lord, knowing that in the Lord your labor is not in vain.* — **1 Corinthians 15:58**

And then, as you tell what you began to experience, God will give you more scriptures that apply, but then they'll be confirmation. Again, what I'm saying, Rana, is that your dream was so powerful that you can definitely go and relay it to the Body of Christ, and somebody will probably have an interpretation.

If you want to be personally confident in releasing this to the people of God, write it down, pray over it, do a word search on the key words, and then be ready to release it to the Body. It could even just be as simple as an email. You can include Paul's experience, where he talks about not being sure if he was caught up in the spirit or not.

Here's How Another Student Who Heard the Dream Interpreted it for Prophecy

When I first heard Rana's dream, I heard the word "paradise." I also heard that the lady had an angelic visitation where God actually sent His angel to get her and take her into a place. Like you said, it was a divine or heavenly experience. The angel was her guide, showing her where he wanted her to go and what was going to happen.

When Rana said she was standing in line, it was like God was saying that it was her time to visit Him in the Holy of Holies. I heard revealing or revelation that God wanted to reveal Himself to her through worship. There was a curtain and I heard the Lord say, "No flesh stands in my presence in the Holy of Holies." And I know that a lot of times in order to go behind the veil, you have to go deep into worship and live a life of worship.

I heard God say as if it were to the Body of Christ that He is calling, "It's our time to go into a deeper part of worship." So we can begin to go in the Holy of Holies to make prophetic petitions on behalf of the people. It seemed like God was calling Rana, or certain types of people, to come before Him, but she said she was lifted up and taken away as if it were not quite time.

Maybe some more things need to take place before she can go into that place with Him behind the veil. But it looked like He wanted to reveal Himself to her because He showed her through the window, but it wasn't quite time because she was taken away.

PROPHETESS DWANN SPEAKING

Rana, what type of prophetic calling is on your life? Tell me more about your prophetic experiences.

RANA SPEAKING

I experience a lot of unexplainable things. I am a convert from Islam. Before I accepted Christ, I was having visions about Christ—the blood of Christ, things like that. When that happened, my visions began to increase. I think God was trying to make himself known, even when I was a child. When I was eleven, I dreamed that I had become a Christian. But never in my mind did I think I'd ever be a Christian, because of the Islamic religion, but Christ set me free. Thank you, Lord!

PROPHETESS DWANN SPEAKING

Rana, you represent those who have been converted, but God is going to do a lot more converting as well. Even those Islamic people in that religion are going to be the ones who are going to be caught up as well. When you know about your background, it makes it even more powerful, because now this isn't just a Word for you or the Body of Christ. This is a word for those converts who need to know and need to be comforted that indeed there is a place for them in Paradise, and that indeed there is a place in His throne room that they can go deeper into as well.

Let me just pray for Rana right now:

Father God, I thank you for Rana. I thank you for everything that you've taken her through. I thank you for the purpose, plan, and destiny that is on her life. I thank you for the prophetic calling that you have upon her now. I thank you for increasing the prophetic on the inside of her, increasing her ability to discern and interpret. I thank you that you are going to call her to help win over those brothers and sisters in Islam who still need to be converted.

I thank you that you are giving her a strategy on how to convert. So even now, I just prophesy a blessing upon her. I decree that no weapon formed against her shall prosper. And I thank you for this dispensation in time that is ordained of you, and she knows and recognizes who she is and all that she's called to do as a Kingdom ambassador.

God, I lift her up and I thank you for your angels being there on assignment 24/7 to war on her behalf and to guard her calling. God, I plead the blood of Jesus over her in the name of Jesus. Amen.

After I had prayed for Rana, another student released this Word of Prophecy to her.

Rana, I heard God say that He has favored you like Esther and that it's truly your time to come behind the veil. It is truly your time to come and make prophetic petition and prophetic intercession on behalf of the Body of Christ. He has called you to a higher place that He has not called everybody, to come to dwell with Him behind the veil.

It is truly your season to begin to go into a deeper dimension in worship. Spend more time in worship and begin to lie before Him and tap into His presence, because there are some things that He wants to share with you face-to-face. He wants you to consecrate more, so you can reach that place.

God says that He has truly favored you and that you are going to experience more angelic visitation. You are going to be able to experience more heavenly visitation and more heavenly experiences. God says He's really going to send angels for you, and they're literally going to lead you into places; later, you are going to find that the places they are leading you are places that you will literally walk into.

In the midnight hour, He's going to take you up out of your house in your sleep and He's going to have you touch foreign ground, then He's going to open up more portals.

God said that He's going to begin to open up portals for you and you're literally going to be transported from one place to another, because God is highly favoring you; you're going to be sent into a window where they are not going to be receptive of female ministers, let alone the gospel.

But God says that He's going to open up portals and that you're going to begin to touch different parts of regions and different countries without even being able to take a flight in the natural. And God says He's even going to open up other portals to be able to transport you back.

In the midnight hour, He's going to take you up out of your house in your sleep and He's going to have you touch foreign ground, then He's going to open up more portals. He's going to take you back, and the angels are going to assist you, escorting you to and fro out of these different countries through these portals. God says He has highly favored you and it's surely your time.

PART THREE

Q & A

What if prophecy comes in the form of a warning and the person rejects it out of fear?

Here's the deal: More often than not, as you see it in the Bible, when warnings were released, they came from prophets of God, apostles, or from God Himself. There was a clear warning, but the people who were being warned were given many opportunities to repent. That's one instance.

The other thing that I find a lot in the Body of Christ is that people take their gifting too seriously. They become so bold in what they're doing that they release it in such a way that brings fear instead of comfort, edification, exhortation, or confirmation. No matter what—whether it's a warning or not—the prophetic word that's released upon you by someone else should confirm, most of the time. But there will be and can be instances where the Word of the Lord will come as a surprise.

If you know for a fact that it really doesn't confirm, or that it's not truly of God, yes, you can reject it. If you're 50/50, you pray over it and put it on a spiritual shelf and you see what happens. If I get a warning, I'm going to take it before God unless I clearly know that it's not of God, because when fear sets in, there's an open door for the demonic to come in even stronger.

So we have to be seasoned in what we're saying and doing in such a way that we're still edifying and comforting the people of God. Again, God may cut you hard, but the thing is, it's still going to bring some sort of comfort and confirmation, because you know God cares for you so much that He would send a warning so that you could get on track.

Can you explain the difference between an open vision and a dream, and how interpretations vary during such?

Normally, with an open vision, you're awake when God downloads something right there in your presence. It may appear as though you're staring into the distance, and unless you are experiencing it, people will just think that you look crazy, or that something's going on. Normally you're either caught up in the Spirit, or He's showing you something that's about to happen.

Many times with dreams, though, they may be predictive; they may also be very metaphorical and symbolic. So if there is a certain person in your life, like a pastor, who is the authority figure in your life (the spiritual authority), he/she may be in your dream and they may not represent themselves—they may represent God.

There's only so much I can say regarding that, but hopefully that helped. Again, your dreams are going to be metaphorical and symbolic. It may seem as though it may be a riddle. It may be something predictive. It may be a real person or a real event, or it may be an open vision where you're literally caught up and your eyes are open and you see what's going on.

What is the difference between words of knowledge and words of prophecy?

Words of knowledge are facts about a person that are unknown to you; however, those facts, as God releases them to you, can be put into a prophecy or put into prayer. Many times, if you're prophetically interceding, God may show you a scene as a seer and it may be from the person's past. That's a word of knowledge that God is going to use for you to connect to their present and/or to their future via the release of the prophetic Word, which is the prophecy.

It's key that you know what to do with it. If you're a prophetic intercessor and God shows you something about a person from their past, more often than not it's for you to intercede several times and just deal with it prophetically in the spirit, unless or until He releases you to minister to that person for whatever reason.

When you see something that is a stronghold that is coming through the leader of your church and keeping the church in bondage, should you tell the leader even if it is operating in them?

Unless God releases you, you should not release it. Your responsibility is to pray, not to try to straighten it out. Now, if God clearly tells you to release it, yes. But more often than not, when God is showing you things like that, it is your responsibility to pray it through: nothing more.

> *You have to be wise as a serpent and harmless as a dove in that situation. I'm not saying that you should never correct, but you have to know without a shadow of a doubt that God has graced you to do the correcting.*

Be very, very careful about releasing words of correction, even if God has shown them to you. Nine times out of ten, He's showing them to you for you to intercede and pray them through, not necessarily to release them. As God is awakening the prophetic to you and ushering you into the office, He's giving you these things because He believes that you are mature enough to handle them.

That maturity means taking it to God in prayer, asking Him what you should do, and getting together with another seasoned prophet to go over it and see what needs to happen—because many times that seasoned prophet can maneuver in the spirit and find out exactly what's going on.

You have to be wise as a serpent and harmless as a dove in that situation. I'm not saying that you should never correct, but you have to know without a shadow of a doubt that God has graced you to do the correcting.

How do you deliver a word of correction?

When God shows a person something, they usually feel that they're the one who needs to correct the issue. Well, that's not necessarily true. You might be the one who's supposed to pray it through, and God may be testing you to see if you are mature enough to deal with what He's showing you. If you have to deliver a word of correction and you're not necessarily a prophet, you first need to go to someone who is ordained or someone who you know operates in the office of a prophet and let them review it.

Then, if they believe that you should release it, I would find a way for them to go with you to release it, because you need that extra backing. You have to deal with the principalities that come against you with your releasing something like that to someone who's walking in another level of authority over you.

So you have to be very, very careful in releasing words of correction. Above all, you want to obey God, but if you're not sure: when in doubt, stick it out, and keep your mouth shut.

Can you suggest a few books for us seers?

I know James Goll has a couple. The *Prophetic Dictionary* by Dr. Paula Price is a great one. I use that. The *Prophet's Handbook* is good as well.

How can a person stir up their prophetic gift if they're just beginning?

One of my great friends says, "Prophets beget prophets." So that means that prophets birth other prophets. You need to get yourself around prophetic people. You need to find yourself a prophetic mentor who can pour into you and help pull out the things of God that are inside of you.

Know that when it's time for you to really be stirred up, God will also usher you into it by giving you dreams and visions and causing you to run into other prophetic people.

Here's a short testimony from one of my prophetic mentees:

> When I came in connection with Ms. Dwann, my level and confidence in the prophetic really went to another level. The activations and the little things she would have me do really made a difference, because she is my mentor and my spiritual mom.
>
> One time, she really had to rebuke me about some things. I was really taken back and discombobulated because I wasn't expecting that to come. But the Lord had led her to do that. So, instantly she shifted and said, "Now prophesy."

I was like, "Are you serious? That's not even my mindset. I'm not even prepared to prophesy."

Then, instantly, when she said it, I literally saw an oak tree being overturned and I saw the roots come right up out of the ground. Instantly, the Lord began to talk to me and tell me what that meant. I began to prophesy it to her and I knew it came from the activations and the little exercises that she would have me do from time-to-time during our mentoring and counseling sessions.

My experience being under a mentor who actually walks in the office of a prophet has increased my confidence level to prophesy, along with my levels of accuracy and boldness as well.

How do you know if you're called in the office of the prophet or if you just have the gift of prophecy?

The gift of prophecy is stirred up when high worship is taking place. It's stirred up when prophetic intercession is taking place. While you're in the office of the prophet, God continuously speaks to you all the time. You see people. You know things.

As a prophet, I can basically release a Word of God as a waterfall on cue. It's who I am. I'm His mouthpiece. More often than not, those who are called to the office of the prophet have gone through hell on earth because of their calling. They go through it for a good four to six years, as God is really inducting them into that office. He shows you how to rely on Him and Him alone.

Conclusion

Where are you in the prophetic? Where are you supposed to be? How are you going to get there? If you are confused about how you are going to get there, please contact me. I would love to mentor you.

.

Activation of Prophecy

Lord I thank you for every seed that has been received on this day as this guidebook has been read.

I thank you that every word that has been read has been received on good fertile ground.

Now, Lord, I come into agreement with your son/daughter and I activate and release the supernatural ability to prophesy.

I thank you, God, for an increase in discernment and revelation as your son/daughter yields to the prophetic power inside them.

I declare and I decree that the ability to prophesy is being activated and stirred up now in Jesus's name. I declare and decree that no weapon formed against biblical prophetics, the spirit of Prophecy, or the ability to prophesy shall prosper in their life.

Even now I awaken the prophesier and call forth the spirit of prophecy that has been lying dormant. I call forth a release of prophetic strategies and revelation that will bring forth results for those you prophesy to.

I thank you, God, that even over the next thirty days, your son/daughter will experience an increase in his/her ability to prophesy and that even the spirit of prophecy will be increased like never before.

Lord, stir up the prophetic gifts like never before. Increase prophetic prayer! Increase prophecy! Increase revelation!

I break every spirit not like you that would try to prevent prophecy from coming forth and that would try to cause no progress when it's time to prophesy.

I push back the hand of the enemy and every demonic strategic plan that would be sent to cause the prophecies to be inaccurate and not hit home. I say that your sons and daughters shall prophesy and shall prophesy well. They shall not be afraid to open their mouths and prophesy. I declare and decree that Bible scriptures will readily come to their minds when it's time to prophesy and that there will be no reservations in prophesying.

I plead the blood of Jesus over your child from the top of his head to the soles of his feet and I thank you for the ability to war for prophecy and prophetic release.

Now, God, I just say: Let your Kingdom Come and your will be done, now in the lives of every believer reading this prophecy activation in the name of Jesus, Amen.

Prophecy Documentation Exercise

Instructions: Now that you have confirmation regarding the practical steps you can implement to release prophecy, let's take it a step further.

I'd like to challenge you to use this guidebook to document prayer and prophecy for the next thirty days.

For the next thirty days, ask God to give you specific people and organizations to pray for. As you pray, take the time to document much of what God is releasing during your prayer time. Then, upon completion of that prayer time, take the time to release a short prophecy and simply document what you are releasing.

If you are led, the next step would be to get that prophecy to that person.

But the most important thing is to make sure you are detailed in your prayer documentation and then to make sure you start each prophecy with a scripture that God has given you to go with your prayer. Then take that scripture and turn it into a prophecy specific to that person.

Sample Entry

December 19, 2014

God led me to pray for Dr. C. In my prayer time, God had me really concentrate on speaking joy and strength in this season.

Here's the scripture God gave me: …

Here's the prophecy I wrote after praying: …

Day 1

_____
_____
_____
_____
_____
_____
_____
_____
_____
_____
_____
_____
_____
_____
_____
_____
_____
_____
_____
_____
_____
_____
_____
_____
_____
_____
_____

Day 2

_____

_____

_____

_____

_____

_____

_____

_____

_____

_____

_____

_____

_____

_____

_____

_____

_____

_____

_____

_____

_____

_____

_____

_____

_____

_____

_____

Day 3

Day 4

_____

_____

_____

_____

_____

_____

_____

_____

_____

_____

_____

_____

_____

_____

_____

_____

_____

_____

_____

_____

_____

_____

_____

_____

_____

_____

_____

_____

Day 5

_____
_____
_____
_____
_____
_____
_____
_____
_____
_____
_____
_____
_____
_____
_____
_____
_____
_____
_____
_____
_____
_____
_____
_____
_____
_____
_____
_____
_____
_____

Day 6

Day 7

_____

_____

_____

_____

_____

_____

_____

_____

_____

_____

_____

_____

_____

_____

_____

_____

_____

_____

_____

_____

_____

_____

_____

_____

_____

_____

_____

_____

_____

_____

_____

_____

Day 8

_____

_____

_____

_____

_____

_____

_____

_____

_____

_____

_____

_____

_____

_____

_____

_____

_____

_____

_____

_____

_____

_____

_____

_____

_____

Day 9

Day 10

Day 11

_____

_____

_____

_____

_____

_____

_____

_____

_____

_____

_____

_____

_____

_____

_____

_____

_____

_____

_____

_____

_____

_____

_____

_____

_____

_____

_____

_____

_____

_____

_____

Day 12

Day 13

_____

_____

_____

_____

_____

_____

_____

_____

_____

_____

_____

_____

_____

_____

_____

_____

_____

_____

_____

_____

_____

_____

_____

_____

Day 14

_____

_____

_____

_____

_____

_____

_____

_____

_____

_____

_____

_____

_____

_____

_____

_____

_____

_____

_____

_____

_____

_____

_____

_____

_____

_____

_____

_____

Day 15

Day 16

Day 17

_____
_____
_____
_____
_____
_____
_____
_____
_____
_____
_____
_____
_____
_____
_____
_____
_____
_____
_____
_____
_____
_____
_____
_____
_____
_____
_____
_____
_____
_____
_____

Day 18

Day 19

Day 20

_____
_____
_____
_____
_____
_____
_____
_____
_____
_____
_____
_____
_____
_____
_____
_____
_____
_____
_____
_____
_____
_____
_____
_____
_____
_____
_____

Day 21

_____
_____
_____
_____
_____
_____
_____
_____
_____
_____
_____
_____
_____
_____
_____
_____
_____
_____
_____
_____
_____
_____
_____
_____
_____
_____
_____
_____
_____
_____

Day 22

Day 23

_____
_____
_____
_____
_____
_____
_____
_____
_____
_____
_____
_____
_____
_____
_____
_____
_____
_____
_____
_____
_____
_____
_____
_____
_____
_____
_____
_____
_____

Day 24

_____

_____

_____

_____

_____

_____

_____

_____

_____

_____

_____

_____

_____

_____

_____

_____

_____

_____

_____

_____

_____

_____

_____

_____

_____

_____

_____

_____

_____

Day 25

_____
_____
_____
_____
_____
_____
_____
_____
_____
_____
_____
_____
_____
_____
_____
_____
_____
_____
_____
_____
_____
_____
_____
_____
_____
_____
_____
_____
_____
_____

Day 26

_____
_____
_____
_____
_____
_____
_____
_____
_____
_____
_____
_____
_____
_____
_____
_____
_____
_____
_____
_____
_____
_____
_____
_____
_____
_____
_____
_____

Day 27

_____

_____

_____

_____

_____

_____

_____

_____

_____

_____

_____

_____

_____

_____

_____

_____

_____

_____

_____

_____

_____

_____

_____

_____

_____

_____

_____

_____

_____

_____

_____

Day 28

Day 29

_____
_____
_____
_____
_____
_____
_____
_____
_____
_____
_____
_____
_____
_____
_____
_____
_____
_____
_____
_____
_____
_____
_____
_____
_____
_____
_____
_____

Day 30

About The Author

Known as a Media Mentor to many, **Dwann Holmes Rollinson** is an award-winning journalist, Emmy-nominated producer, and marketing executive called to leverage leaders into new levels of Kingdom Manifestation. Rollinson combines her 20+ year media background with ministerial insight to show God's apostles, prophets, evangelists, pastors, and teachers how to easily evangelize on- and offline.

As FOUNDER of the **GLOBAL INSTITUTE OF CHURCH & MARKETPLACE PROPHETS,** Dwann is a Prophetic Authority to the nations called to set order and build systems of accountability for God's Kingdom mouthpieces across the world.

As Executive Pastor of The Worship Place in Jacksonville, Florida, Rollinson stands beside her husband, **Bishop Harold Rollinson.** Together they have founded Global Apostolic Prophetic (G.A.P.) Kingdom Builders

Dwann is also a member of New Era Apostleship Restitution (N.E.A.R.) founded by Dr. Paula Price, and sits on the High Council of the organization.

Whether in the pulpit or auditorium, Apostle Dwann walks in miracles, signs, and wonders, bringing healing, hope, and prophetic revelation to all, particularly those called to Marketplace Ministry & Prophetics. **"America's DEAN of Divine Design,"** Apostle Dwann helps Christian divorcees and overwhelmed college students conquer crisis to move from defeat to destiny! (DwannSpeaks.com)

In April 2001, *Ebony* Magazine named her one of thirty future leaders of America aged 30 and under. As a former broadcast journalist, she was accustomed to reporting the story, but now she's called to tell her personal story regarding Christians and divorce: A story that she speaks of from her experience of how her FAITH led her through a recent unexpected crisis to a steady place in the midst of the storm, which is detailed in her upcoming book, *Life Interrupted: Seven Key Strategies To Overcoming Difficult Times.* Now, Dwann combines her pastoral counseling skills with her skills as a leadership trainer to help people of all backgrounds WIN THROUGH CRISIS.

To find out more about Dwann's personal prophetic ministry, visit www.ProphetDwann.com and follow Dwann on social media **@ProphetDwann.** To find out more about Dwann's prophetic school, visit **www.GlobalPropheticInstitute.com**

Because many people ask how to bring Apostle Dwann to speak at their events, here's information you'll appreciate. Apostle Dwann's ministry programs are revolutionary and full of revelation!

Apostle Dwann is available as a *Keynote speaker* for:

• Global, National, Regional & State Prophetic & Apostolic Conferences
• "Teach Me How To Prophesy" Seminars & Workshops
• "Signs, Wonders & Miracles" Seminars & Workshops
• "Boost The Prophetic In You" Seminars & Workshops
• "Prophetic Training & Mentorship Programs & Conferences
• "5-Fold Ministry Leadership Seminars, Workshops & Conferences
• Launching A Global, Regional or Local, Company of Prophets
• THE ART OF PROPHETIC INTERCESSION Seminars & Workshops

Call Today to Reserve
Apostle Dwann
For Your Next Prophetic Event!

To Bring Prophet Dwann and her Powerful Ministry to support your Event, Conference or Program:

Visit: www.ProphetDwann.com
Email: info@ProphetDwann.com
Call Toll-Free: 877-595-9117

To find out more about Apostle Dwann's Prophetic Training Marketplace Ministry visit:
www.GlobalProphetInstitute.com
or to learn more
about her Business Leadership Program visit
www.DwannSpeaks.com

Apostle
Dwann Rollinson
FOLLOW ME @PROPHETDWANN

THE GLOBAL INSTITUTE (ASSOCIATION) OF CHURCH AND MARKETPLACE PROPHETS exists as an international professional company of prophets charged with educating, enlightening and empowering those chosen by God to the Prophetic Ministry. The mission of the **Global Institute of Church and Marketplace Prophets** (*GICMP*) is to provide support, prophetic counseling and education to all Christian Prophets around the world, whether called to the church or the marketplace. GICMP's charge is to also exist as a bridge between Pastors and Prophets while also providing **prophetic** organizational structure to churches and marketplace organizations (*businesses*)

WWW.GLOBALPROPHETICINSTITUTE.COM

Apostle
Dwann Rollinson
FOLLOW ME @PROPHETDWANN
WWW.PROPHETDWANN.COM

JOIN THE PROPHETS FOR PRAYER
EVERY *Monday, Wednesday and Friday*

MARKETPLACE MONDAY Prayer for Business People
WISDOM WEDNESDAY for Teachers call
5-FOLD FRIDAY Prayer for Ministry Leaders
Conference Number: 712-432-1630 Access Code: 418609 Time: 7-7:15AM EST

1 on 1 Private Prophecy, Prayer & Deliverance Ministry
www.GetProphecyNow.com

About SermonToBook.Com

SermonToBook.com began with a simple belief: that sermons should be touching lives, *not* collecting dust. That's why we turn sermons into high-quality books that are accessible to people all over the globe.

Turning your sermon or sermon series into a book exposes more people to God's Word, better equips you for counseling, accelerates future sermon prep, adds credibility to your ministry, and even helps make ends meet during tight times.

John 21:25 tells us that the world itself couldn't contain the books that would be written about the work of Jesus Christ. Our mission is to try anyway, because in Heaven, there will no longer be a need for sermons or books. Our time is now.

If God so leads you, we'd love to work with you on your sermon or sermon series.

Visit www.sermontobook.com to learn more.

Made in the USA
Lexington, KY
09 May 2018